Skyscrapers are buildings that seem to scrape the sky

Skyscrapers

Janet Halfmann

A⁺
Smart Apple Media

COPYRIGHT

❖ Published by Smart Apple Media

1980 Lookout Drive, North Mankato, Minnesota 56003

Designed by Rita Marshall

Copyright © 2003 Smart Apple Media. International copyright reserved in
all countries. No part of this book may be reproduced in any form without
written permission from the publisher.

Printed in the United States of America

❖ Photographs by Corbis (Bettmann Archive), Richard Cummins,
Steven Dahlman, Bruce Leighty, Tom Myers, James P. Rowan

❖ Library of Congress Cataloging-in-Publication Data

Halfmann, Janet. Skyscrapers / by Janet Halfmann. p. cm. — (Structures)

Includes index.

Summary: Briefly describes the history and construction of skyscrapers, tall
buildings which were first built in the United States.

❖ ISBN 1-58340-145-8

1. Skyscrapers—Juvenile literature. [1. Skyscrapers]. I. Title. II. Structures
(North Mankato, Minn.)

NA6230 .H34 2002   720'.483—dc21   2001049970

❖ First Edition 9 8 7 6 5 4 3 2 1

Skyscrapers

Scraping the Sky

Skyscrapers—the world's tallest buildings—seem to scrape the sky. The first one rose only 10 stories, or floors. Today's skyscrapers tower 100 stories or more. Skyscrapers were first built in the United States. But these towering buildings now rule skylines around the world. ❖ Skyscrapers provide a lot of space for offices and housing on a small amount of land. That is important in today's crowded cities, such as London and New York. In 2001, the two New York

Many skyscrapers have unique decorative touches

skyscrapers known as the World Trade Center were destroyed

by **terrorists**. Before that, though, the towers included

offices, shops, restaurants, a hotel, a railway station, and

parking lots. Each day, 50,000 workers and 200,000 visitors

filled the Center's twin towers.

From the Bottom Up

Architects and engineers work together to create a

skyscraper. An architect decides on the shape and materials. An

engineer makes the skyscraper safe against fires, earthquakes,

and wind. ❖ Skyscrapers are built on an underground

foundation. When there is solid rock below ground, workers

hammer strong, steel columns down into the rock. These

columns are called piles. In areas that have soft soil, workers

Skyscrapers start with a strong steel frame

At night, skyscrapers light up a city's skyline

may pour a concrete slab that keeps the building from sinking.

Above ground, workers build a skeleton frame made of

steel columns and beams. The frame holds up the skyscraper,

much as a skeleton holds up a person's body. When workers raise the last beam of a skyscraper's frame, they attach a fir tree or flag for good luck. ❖ As the **To keep them from swaying too much in the wind, some skyscrapers are built with heavy weights in their tops.**

frame goes up, other workers lay the floors. The walls, which

get hung on the frame like curtains, are called **curtain walls**.

Walls might be made of **marble** like those in the skyscraper

called First Canadian Place in Toronto, Ontario. The walls of a

skyscraper called PPG Place in Pittsburgh, Pennsylvania, are

made of glass that glows like a fairy-tale castle at night. ❖

People who build skyscrapers must wear safety equipment

Meanwhile, inside the building, workers install elevators, water pipes, electrical wires, telephone and computer lines, and heating, air conditioning, and security systems. They paint and decorate the rooms. When they reach the top floor, the skyscraper is done!

A Fiery Start

Why was the first skyscraper built? After a huge fire destroyed much of Chicago, Illinois, in 1871, thousands of homes and businesses had to be rebuilt. But land was expensive. So designers decided to build up. ❖ William Le

Baron Jenney was one of those designers. One evening, he

watched his wife plop a heavy book on top of a metal birdcage.

To his surprise, the birdcage did not bend at all! Why not use

Skyscrapers are built in many sizes and colors

a cage-like metal frame to hold up a tall building, he thought.

❖ Jenney used his idea to build the 10-story Home

Insurance Building in 1885. The metal frame worked so well

for the first skyscraper that it is still used

today. Jenney also used another impor-

tant invention of the time—the elevator.

Elevators allowed people to ride to the

Japan's Landmark Tower has the world's fastest elevator. It rockets up to the 69th floor in 40 seconds!

higher floors instead of climbing many stairs. Soon, more

skyscrapers went up in other large cities.

The world's first skyscraper was 10 stories tall

Higher and Higher

For a while, Chicago had the world's tallest skyscrapers. But New York City soon took the lead. The 102-story Empire State Building, which was 1,250 feet (381 m) tall, held the record as the tallest building for 41 years. The World Trade Center took the title in 1972 but did not hold it for long.

Chicago's Sears Tower has floor space equal to the space on 65 football fields.

In 1974, Chicago soared back on top with the 110-story Sears Tower, which stood 1,454 feet (443 m) tall. Then, in 1998, the

The Sears Tower is the world's second-tallest building

spires of the Petronas Towers in Kuala Lumpur, Malaysia, were built. They were 29 feet (9 m) higher than the Sears Tower. It was the first time a skyscraper outside the United States was the world's tallest building. ❖

Today, architects in Japan are planning to build Sky City 1,000. This will be a super-high-rise city that will include schools,

Some skyscrapers have helicopter landing pads, gardens, or swimming pools on their rooftops.

parks, apartments, offices, and stores. One day, people may be able to spend their entire lives in that "city in the clouds."

Things on the ground look small from a skyscraper's roof

Build a Skyscraper

Skyscrapers can look like tall boxes, round towers, triangles, or even a stack of diamonds. You can build your own miniature skyscraper.

What You Need

Cardboard (cereal boxes work well)   Paper
Three-ounce (89 ml) paper cups   Tape
Crayons or markers   Scissors

What You Do

1. Cut the cardboard in equal pieces about six inches (15 cm) by eight inches (20 cm).
2. Lay a piece of cardboard on a hard, flat surface. This is your foundation.
3. Put a cup, upside-down, near each corner for the frame.
4. Lay another piece of cardboard on top of the cups.
5. Alternate cups and cardboard, building your skyscraper taller and taller.
6. Decorate paper with crayons or markers for curtain walls. Include windows and doors.
7. Tape the walls to the cardboard.

To build skyscrapers of different shapes, cut the cardboard pieces into circles or triangles.

Most skyscrapers are square or rectangular in shape

Index

Words to Know

curtain walls (KUR-tun wallz)—the thin outside walls of a skyscraper

foundation (fown-DAY-shun)—the strong base on which a skyscraper rests

marble (MAR-bull)—a shiny and attractive kind of rock

skeleton frame (SKELL-uh-tun fraym)—the steel framework around which a sky-scraper is built

spires (SPYRZ)—tall, thin structures that narrow to a point; they are built on the tops of buildings

terrorists (TARE-or-ists)—people who use violence to scare other groups of people

Read More

Hunter, Ryan Ann. *Into the Sky*. New York: Holiday House, 1998.

Ingoglia, Gina. *The Big Book of Real Skyscrapers*. New York: Grosset & Dunlap, 1989.

Landau, Elaine. *Skyscrapers*. New York: Children's Press, 2001.

Internet Sites

The Empire State Building

http://www.esbnyc.com

The Skyscraper Museum

http://www.skyscraper.org

Sears Tower

http://sears-tower.com

Skyscrapers.com

http://skyscrapers.com